Williamson v. Shrackle

Case File

Williamson v. Shrackle

Case File

adapted from a case file by Professors Kenneth Broun
and James H. Seckinger

adaptation by

Professor Molly O'Brien
Steven Friedman, Esq.
Kevin L. Prins

NATIONAL INSTITUTE FOR TRIAL ADVOCACY

Reproduction Permission
National Institute for Trial Advocacy
Notre Dame Law School
Notre Dame, Indiana 46556
(800) 225-6482 FAX (219) 282-1263
E-mail: nita.1@nd.edu
Web site: www.nita.org

O'Brien, Molly, Steven Friedman, Kevin L. Prins, *Williamson v. Shrackle* (NITA 1999).

Adapted from: Broun, Kenneth S. and James H. Seckinger, *Potter v. Shrackle and the Shrackle Construction Company* (NITA 1992).

ISBN 978-1-55681-680-2

Wolters Kluwer

Official co-publisher of NITA.
WKLegaledu.com/NITA

WILLIAMSON v. SHRACKLE

TABLE OF CONTENTS

INTRODUCTION

INTRODUCTION

This is a civil negligence action brought in the Nita state court by Professor Fergus D. Williamson against Charles T. Shrackle and the Shrackle Construction Company. Williamson claims that Shrackle negligently drove the company's pickup truck, striking Williamson as he was crossing the street, causing him severe injury and continuing disability. Williamson claims that Shrackle was acting in the course of the Shrackle Construction Company's business at the time of the event.

Shrackle admits striking Professor Williamson, but claims that he was crossing in the middle of the street, rather than in the pedestrian crosswalk, and that he did not look before entering the street in the path of Mr. Shrackle's pickup truck. Defendants deny that Shrackle was negligent and allege contributory negligence on the part of the plaintiff, Professor Williamson.

The applicable law is contained statutes and the proposed jury instructions set forth at the end of the file.

All years in these materials are stated in the following form:

- YR-0 indicates the actual year in which the case is being tried (i.e., the present year);
- YR-1 indicates the next preceding year (please use the actual year);
- YR-2 indicates the second preceding year (please use the actual year,) etc.

Electronic exhibits can be found at the following website:

http://bit.ly/1P20Jea
Password: Williamson

SPECIAL INSTRUCTIONS FOR USE AS A FULL TRIAL

Issues for Trial

This case file may be used for a full trial on the issue of liability only or on the issues of both liability and damages. If used solely for the issue of liability, the proposed jury instructions should be modified accordingly by deleting instructions 14, 15 and 16. The testimony of Dr. McKellar Rogers, Paris Fisher, Pat Daniels, and Cameron Sawyer relate only to damages issues. These witnesses should not be called in a trial on liability only. The testimony of Wyeth Waring relates primarily to damages. Some plaintiffs may wish to call Wyeth Waring during a trial on liability to explain who the plaintiff is and why he was on the corner where the accident occurred. If the constraints of the trial require a limited number of witnesses, the parties should prepare a statement identifying the plaintiff for the court to read to the jury.

Witnesses

When this case file is used for a full trial, the following witnesses are available:

For the plaintiff:

	Liability:	Officer Robin Young Taylor Kelly Pat Marshall
	Damages:	Wyeth Waring, Esq. Dr. McKellar Rogers Paris Fisher

For the defendants:

	Liability:	Charles Shrackle Lee Mallory Jesse Johnson Chris Johnson
	Damages:	Pat Daniels Cameron Sawyer

Plaintiff Fergus Williamson and Defendant Charles Shrackle are men. All of the other witness roles may be played by either men or women. Plaintiff Williamson must be considered unavailable for all purposes.

IN THE CIRCUIT COURT OF
DARROW COUNTY, NITA
CIVIL DIVISION

Fergus D. Williamson, by and through his guardian ad litem, Wyeth Waring, Plaintiff, v. Charles T. Shrackle and The Shrackle Construction Company, Defendants.	))))))))))))	COMPLAINT

Plaintiff for his Complaint against Defendants alleges:

FIRST CLAIM FOR RELIEF

1. That at all times hereinafter mentioned, Plaintiff was, and still is, a resident of Darrow County, Nita.

2. That at all times hereinafter mentioned, Defendant Charles T. Shrackle was, and still is, a resident of Darrow County, Nita, and the Defendant Shrackle Construction Company was, and still is, doing business in Darrow County, Nita.

3. That Wyeth Waring is the duly appointed guardian ad litem of Plaintiff Fergus Williamson, and is fully authorized to bring this action on plaintiff's behalf.

4. That on May 8, YR-2, at about 3:30 p.m., Fergus Williamson was walking in an eastwardly direction across Mattis Avenue at the intersection of Mattis and Kirby Avenues in Nita City, Nita.

5. At this time and place Defendant Charles T. Shrackle was driving a white YR-9 Chevrolet pickup truck which struck Fergus Williamson, causing him serious injuries.

6. That the pickup truck driven by Defendant Charles T. Shrackle was owned by the Defendant Shrackle Construction Company, and at the time Fergus Williamson was struck by the truck, Charles T. Shrackle was performing duties for and acting on behalf of the Shrackle Construction Company.

7. That Defendant Charles T. Shrackle was driving the truck in a careless, negligent, and reckless manner, and in violation of his duties under Nita Revised Statutes 89-12(4) (1968) to exercise due care to avoid striking the pedestrian Fergus Williamson who was then lawfully crossing the street.

8. That Defendant Charles T. Shrackle carelessly, negligently, and in violation of Nita Revised Statutes 89-12(4) (1968) failed to keep a proper lookout, to heed the fact that Fergus Williamson was crossing the street in the immediate path of his truck, or to take any action to avoid striking Fergus Williamson.

9. That Defendant Charles T. Shrackle carelessly, negligently, and in violation of Nita Revised Statutes 89-12(4) (1968) failed to give proper warning of the sudden and unexpected approach of his truck either by sounding the horn or giving any other signal or warning.

10. That Defendant Charles T. Shrackle's negligence caused Fergus Williamson to suffer severe and permanent injuries to his brain and soft tissues within the skull. As a result, he has experienced and will experience in the future great pain and suffering, both mental and physical, and continuing permanent partial physical and mental disability, loss of earning capacity, and loss of capacity to enjoy life.

11. That Defendant Charles T. Shrackle's negligence caused Fergus Williamson to incur special damages for medical, hospital, surgical care, and loss of income; and plaintiff will sustain additional special damages therefore in the future.

JURY DEMAND

Plaintiff demands a trial by jury in this action.

MADDEN & JAMES

by THOMAS MADDEN

Attorneys for Plaintiff
Suite 720, Nita Bank Building
Nita City, Nita 99994
(721) 555-0003

DATED: April 7, YR-1

Return on Summons

I hereby certify that the above complaint was personally served on Charles T. Shrackle at his office at the Shrackle Construction Company, Nita City, Nita 99996.

James Bell
James Bell
Speedy Subpoena & Process, Inc.

IN THE CIRCUIT COURT OF
DARROW COUNTY, NITA
CIVIL DIVISION

Fergus D. Williamson, by and through his guardian ad litem, Wyeth Waring, Plaintiff, v. Charles T. Shrackle and Shrackle Construction Company, Defendants.	)	ANSWER

Defendants for their Answer to Plaintiff's Complaint:

1. Admit the allegations contained in paragraphs 1, 2, and 3.

2. Admit that on May 8, YR-2, at or about 3:30 p.m., Fergus Williamson was crossing Mattis Avenue somewhere near the intersection of Kirby and Mattis Avenues. Defendants deny all other allegations in paragraph 4.

3. Admit that Charles T. Shrackle was driving a pickup truck which struck Fergus Williamson. Defendants lack any knowledge of the nature or extent of Plaintiff's injuries, if any, and therefore deny the allegations of serious injury.

4. Admit that the pickup truck driven by Charles T. Shrackle was owned by the Shrackle Construction Company. Defendants deny all other allegations in paragraph 6.

5. Deny the allegations contained in paragraphs 7-9 and have no knowledge of the allegations in paragraph 10 and therefore deny them.

FIRST AFFIRMATIVE DEFENSE

6. Any injuries sustained or suffered by Fergus Williamson at the time and place mentioned in the Complaint were caused, in whole or in part, or were contributed to, by the negligence of Fergus Williamson and not by any negligence of Charles T. Shrackle.

SECOND AFFIRMATIVE DEFENSE

7. Fergus Williamson violated Nita Revised Statutes 89-12(4) (1968) by failing to cross the street in the marked pedestrian crosswalk, to keep a proper lookout for vehicles using the roadway and to yield the right of way to any such vehicles.

WHEREFORE, Defendants demand that judgment be entered in favor of the Defendants with the costs and disbursements of this action.

PIERCE, JOHNSON & CLARK

by

Judith Clark

Attorneys for Defendants
Nita National Bank Plaza
Nita City, Nita 99994
(721) 555-6207

DATED: April 16, YR-1

Certificate of Service

I hereby certify that a copy of the above Answer was placed in the United States Mail, postage prepaid, addressed to the law firm of Madden & James, Suite 720, Nita Bank Building, Nita City, Nita 99994.

Marilyn Maxwell

Marilyn Maxwell
350 Court Place
Nita City, Nita 99993
(721) 555-4250

DEPT. OF TRANSPORTATION
BUREAU OF SAFETY PROGRAMMING AND ANALYSIS
T & S BUILDING, NITA CITY, NITA

POLICE ACCIDENT REPORT

REPORTABLE ☐
NON-REPORTABLE ☐
HAZARDOUS MATERIALS ☐

1. INCIDENT NUMBER	2. AGENCY NAME	3. STATION PRECINCT
0717	Nita City Police Dept.	12th

4. INVESTIGATING OFFICER	BADGE NO.	5. DATE OF REPORT	6. APPROVED BY	7. DATE APPROVED
Robin Young	7319	5-9-YR-2	BW	5-9-YR-2

8. DATE	9. DAY	10. TIME	11. COUNTY	12. CODE	13. PATROL ZONE
5-8-YR2	FRIDAY	3:28 pm	Darrow	01	7

14. NO. VEHICLES	15. NO. KILLED	16. NO. INJURED	17. MUNICIPALITY	18. CODE
1	0	1		01

UNIT NO 1

19. OPERATOR LICENSE NO.	CLASS	20. STATE	21. SEX	22. D.O.B.	23. LEGALLY PARKED	24. ILLEGALLY PARKED	25. HIT & RUN
V311-5114-1161-N	1		M	8-13-YR-33			

26. NAME	ADDRESS
Charles T. SHRACKLE	1701 W. Johnston, Nita City

27. OWNER NAME	ADDRESS
Same	

28. VEHICLE TITLE NO.	29. YEAR	30. MAKE	31. MODEL	32. REGISTRATION NO.	33. STATE
113457-6	YR-9	Chevy	Pick-up	237952B	Nita

34. INSURANCE CO. NAME	35. INSURANCE CO. CODE	36. INSURANCE POLICY NO.
Boston Casualty	59	FA 606560

37. TOWED TO	38. TOWED BY
Destination	

UNIT NO 2

19. OPERATOR LICENSE NO.	CLASS	20. STATE	21. SEX	22. D.O.B.	23. LEGALLY PARKED	24. ILLEGALLY PARKED	25. HIT & RUN
PedesTRIAN			M	4-1-YR-62			

26. NAME	ADDRESS
Fergus Williamson	718 Flower Dr, Nita City

27. OWNER NAME	ADDRESS

28. VEHICLE TITLE NO.	29. YEAR	30. MAKE	31. MODEL	32. REGISTRATION NO.	33. STATE

34. INSURANCE CO. NAME	35. INSURANCE CO. CODE	36. INSURANCE POLICY NO.

37. TOWED TO	38. TOWED BY

39. DESCRIPTION OF DAMAGED PROPERTY:	40. OWNER

PRINCIPAL ROAD / **INTERSECTING ROAD**

41. ROUTE NO. OR STREET NAME	42. SPEED LIMIT	43. CIRCLE IF ONE WAY	44. ROUTE NO. OR STREET NAME	45. SPEED LIMIT
Mattis	30	N S E W	KIRBY	30

IF NOT AT INTERSECTION	46. NEAREST CROSS ROUTE OR MILEPOST NO.	47. DIR. FROM ACCIDENT SITE	48. DISTANCE FROM ACCIDENT SITE	49. WAS DISTANCE
		N (S) E W	30′	☐ MEASURED? ☒ ESTIMATED?

50. ILLUMINATION	51. WEATHER	52. ROAD SURFACE	53. TRAFFIC CONTROL DEVICE TYPE
1. DAWN OR DUSK 2. DAYLIGHT 3. DARK (ST. LIGHTS ON) 4. DARK (NO ST. LIGHTS)	0. NO ADVERSE CONDITIONS 1. RAINING 2. SLEET, HAIL, ETC. 3. SNOWING 4. FOG, SMOKE, ETC. 5. RAINING AND FOGGY	1. DRY 2. WET 3. MUDDY 4. SNOW OR ICE	0. NO CONTROLS 1. FLASHING TRAFFIC SIGNAL 2. TRAFFIC SIGNAL 3. STOP SIGN 4. YIELD SIGN 5. RR CROSSING CONTROLS 6. POLICE OFFICER OR FLAGMAN 7. FLASHING SCHOOL ZONE SIGN 8. OTHER
2	0	1	PRIN ROAD: 2 / INT ROAD: 2

54. WITNESS(ES) NAME	ADDRESS
A < Jesse Johnson / Chris Johnson	1010 W. Kirby #15, City
B - Taylor Kelly	1910 Elder Lane, City

55. INJURED TAKEN TO:	BY:
City Hospital	Investigating officer

56. USE CODES ON OVERLAY SHEET TO COMPLETE BLOCKS A THRU N OF THIS SECTION

A	B	C	D	E	F	G	NAME	ADDRESS	H	I	J	K	L	M	N

57. DIAGRAM

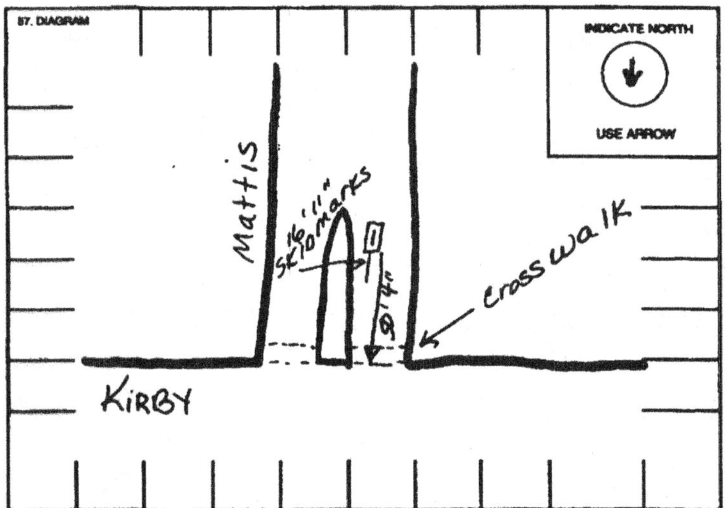

Number of Lanes on Principal Road:

58. NARRATIVE

#1 was south bound on Mattis after turning left from Kirby. He then struck pedestrian approx. 30' south of pedes. crosswalk

#1 said he didn't see pedestrian until after he struck him. Witness A had been in car just in front of #1 and saw pedestrian going across street westbound. Witness did not see actual contact.

Witness B. later called station and said pedestrian was in cross walk.

67. VIOLATIONS INDICATED UNIT NO. 1 | 69. CITATION(S) UNIT NO. 1

68. VIOLATIONS INDICATED UNIT NO. 2 | 70. CITATION(S) UNIT NO. 2

INCIDENT NUMBER:

VEHICLE NUMBER

1		2
10	59. AUTO/TRUCK BODY TYPE 01 - CONVERTIBLE 02 - 2 DR HARDTOP 03 - 4 DR HARDTOP 04 - 2 DR SEDAN 05 - 4 DR SEDAN 06 - STA. WAGON 07 - LIMOUSINE 08 - OTHER AUTO 09 - JEEP, ETC. 10 - PICK-UP 11 - VAN (NOT MOVING VAN OR HORSE VAN) 12 - TOW TRUCK 13 - OTHER SINGLE UNIT TRUCK 14 - TRACTOR (CAB ONLY) 15 - TRACTOR TRAILER 16 - OTHER TRUCK BODY	
01	60. INITIAL POINT OF IMPACT 00 - NONE 07 - TOP 08 - UNDERCARRIAGE 09 - TOWED UNIT 99 - UNKNOWN (01, 02, 03, 07, 04, 05, 06)	
1	61. VEHICLE DAMAGE SEVERITY 0 - NONE 1 - LIGHT 2 - MODERATE 3 - SEVERE	
1	62. WAS TOWING REQUIRED? 0 - NO 1 - YES	
30	63. ESTIMATED TRAVEL SPEED 00 - NONE (STOPPED/PARKED) 01-97 - CODE ACTUAL SPEED 98 - 98 OR GREATER 99 - UNKNOWN	
1	64. VEHICLE GRADIENT 1 - LEVEL ROADWAY 2 - UPHILL 3 - DOWNHILL	
00	65. SPECIAL USAGE 00 - NONE 01 - PUPIL TRANSPORT 02 - FIRE VEHICLE 03 - AMBULANCE 04 - OTHER EMERGENCY VEHICLE 05 - STATE POLICE VEHICLE 06 - DOT VEHICLE 07 - OTHER STATE GOV'T VEHICLE 08 - MUNICIPAL GOV'T VEHICLE 09 - OTHER MUNICIPAL GOV'T VEHICLE 10 - FEDERAL GOV'T VEHICLE 11 - TAXI 12 - TOWING CAR 13 - TOWING TRUCK 14 - TOWING UTILITY TRAILER 15 - TOWING MOBILE/MODULAR HOME 16 - TOWING CAMPER	
00	66. HAZARDOUS SUBSTANCE TYPE - FROM PLACARD 00 - NOT APPLICABLE 01 - NON-FLAMMABLE GAS 02 - COMBUSTIBLE 03 - ORGANIC PEROXIDE 04 - CORROSIVE 05 - EXPLOSIVE "A" 06 - OXYGEN 07 - POISON 08 - EXPLOSIVE "B" 09 - CHLORINE 10 - OXIDIZER 11 - POISON GAS 12 - FUEL OIL 13 - DANGEROUS 14 - RADIOACTIVE 15 - FLAMMABLE SOLID -W 16 - FLAMMABLE 17 - FLAMMABLE GAS 18 - FLAMMABLE SOLID 19 - GASOLINE 20 - BLASTING AGENTS 98 - OTHER	

FOR ALCOHOL TEST TYPES BLOCKS 72 AND 75 USE THE FOLLOWING CODES: 1 - BLOOD 2 - BREATH 3 - URINE 4 - TEST REFUSED 5 - OTHER CHEMICAL

71. NAME	72. TYPE	73. RESULT	74. NAME	75. TYPE	76. RESULT	77. IS INVESTIGATION COMPLETE?
		___%			___%	Yes

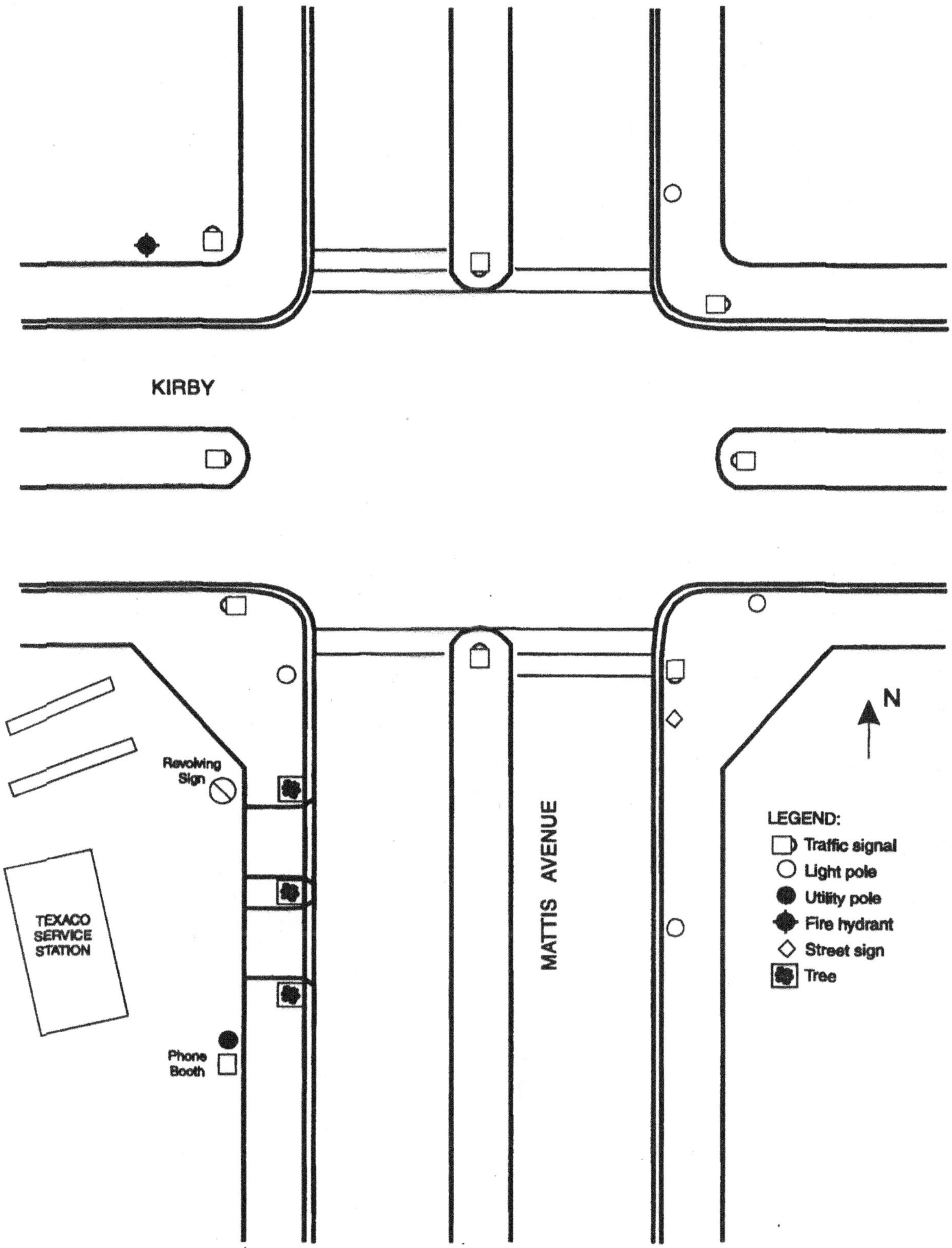

DRAWING OF INTERSECTION

STATEMENT OF TAYLOR KELLY*

Re: Fergus D. Williamson
Date of Accident: May 8,YR-2

My name is Taylor Kelly. I live at 1910 Elder Lane, Nita City 99992. Telephone 555-1213.

On May 8, YR-2, at approximately 3:20 p.m., I was driving my car and was stopped in the eastwardly northbound lane on Mattis Avenue at the intersection of Mattis Avenue and Kirby Avenue in Nita City. The light had turned yellow as I approached the intersection, and I came to a complete stop with the front of my car just south of the crosswalk.

Just as I stopped, a small boy ran across the street from the west to east and barely avoided being struck by a car making a left turn from Kirby onto Mattis heading south. When he reached the sidewalk, I heard the crossing guard who was standing on the southeast corner of the intersection speak to the boy and say something to the effect that,"You have got to watch for cars."

I then saw a thin man with white sideburns, wearing grey sweat pants, a yellow T-shirt, and white running shoes on the west side of Mattis Avenue. He was just stepping off the curb and starting to cross the street when I saw him. At that time the man was walking at a normal gait and was not running. He was definitely in the crosswalk, and I saw him take two or three steps.

I then glanced back up at the light, and at that time I heard a thud. I looked up and saw the man flying through the air and then land with arms outstretched on the front of the truck. He then went backward as if doing a backward somersault and fell under the truck. At that time I thought to myself,"My God, stop, don't run over him again." The truck driver appeared to be looking around immediately after the impact as though looking to see what he had hit.

The truck stopped at a point approximately fifty feet south of the south line of Kirby. At the point where the truck stopped the man was almost entirely underneath the truck. I definitely heard the thud before I heard the sound of any brakes shrieking. At the time of the thud the front of the truck was about even with the front of my car and was not completely straightened out from making the left turn.

The sun at the time of the occurrence was extremely bright and was coming from a westwardly direction, and I had to shade my eyes when I looked back to the scene after the truck came to a stop.

After the truck stopped, a man ran out of the nearby gas station and the driver of the truck got out and went around to the front of the vehicle.

I do not know the Williamson family, Mr. Shrackle, the driver of the truck, or anyone at Shrackle Construction Co.

I stayed at the scene for a couple of minutes, and then I left. I had an appointment for a hair cut in the Lincolnshire Shopping Plaza.

The following morning at approximately 8:30, I read about the accident in the Nita City newspaper. The newspaper stated that the man was running and was approximately thirty feet south of the crosswalk at the time he was hit by the truck. I then telephoned the police and advised them that I had witnessed the accident, and that the man was in the crosswalk and that he was not running.

I have read the above and foregoing statement consisting of two pages and the same is true and correct.

Signed: Taylor Kelly Date: 5/12/YR-2
Taylor Kelly

Witness: Robin Young Date: 5/12/YR-2
Officer Robin Young
Nita City Police Department

---

* This statement was given to Officer Robin Young at the Nita City Police Department on May 12, YR-2.

Statement of Pat Marshall

Statement of Pat Marshall

I am the owner of Pat Marshall's Texaco, 1601 Mattis, Nita City, Nita. I was working at the station on May 8, YR-2.

At approximately 3:30 pm May 8, YR-2, I was looking out the ~~west~~ NORTH bay of my station when I saw a white-haired man walking on the west side of Kirby Ave. He was walking east on the sidewalk. I looked at an employee to say something and then I heard a thump. I looked out and saw a pickup truck carrying a body on the front of it. I sent an employee out to see if he could be of help while I called the police. I went out to see if I could help and saw it was the same man I'd seen earlier walking east on Kirby. He was lying on the pavement.

Signed Pat Marshall

Witness: Joseph Lucey
May 12, YR-2

Editor's Note: Marshall's station is located on the southwest corner of Kirby and Mattis. This statement was taken by Joseph Lucey, an adjuster for the defendant's insurance carrier, at Marshall's station on May 12, YR-2, at about 11 A.M. The statement was written by Mr. Lucey. The signature and the correction are in Marshall's handwriting.

STATEMENT OF CHRIS JOHNSON*

On May 8, YR-2, at approximately 3:30 p.m. at the corner of Kirby and Mattis, I was stopped on the west side of Kirby waiting for the light to change to green. A man in a white pickup truck was in the left-hand lane on the opposite side of Kirby with his left turn signal on as he was waiting to turn south on Mattis. The light changed to green, he waited until I had passed and with the light still green he turned south on Mattis.

I actually didn't see him hit the man, who I later found out was Professor Williamson, but the truck could not have been going fast because I was only a few feet from the intersection when my daughter said, "Hey, I think someone has been hit." We immediately turned around and went back to the accident.

When we went back to the intersection, I saw the man with white sideburns lying underneath the white pickup truck. It was then that I learned the driver of the white pickup truck was Charles Shrackle of the Shrackle Construction Company and the man who was hit by the truck was Professor Williamson.

I have read the above and it is my statement.

Signed *Chris Johnson* Date: 5/9/YR-2

Chris Johnson

Witness *Joseph Lucey* Date: 5/9/YR-2

Joseph Lucey

---

* This statement was given to Joseph Lucey, an adjuster for the defendant's insurance carrier, at the Johnsons' home on May 9, YR-2.

STATEMENT OF JESSE JOHNSON*

As I was coming home from school on May 8, YR-2, about 3:30 p.m., we were headed east on Kirby Avenue. We were stopped at the intersection and a man in a white pickup truck was on the opposite side of Kirby in the left lane ready to make a left turn and go south on Mattis. We crossed the intersection, the man in the white truck waited for us to cross, and then he proceeded to turn the corner. A white-haired man was about twenty feet south of the crosswalk, on the median--facing my friends and with his back to me. He then stepped off the median into the path of the white truck. He was a little ways into the street when he was struck. I saw his baseball cap fly up into the air and heard the screech of brakes.

I called out that I thought someone had been hit, and we went back to the intersection. I saw the man who was hit lying underneath the front of the white truck.

The police came and I found out that the driver of the white truck was Charles Shrackle and the man was Professor Williamson.

I am ten years old. My next birthday is next year.

I have read the above and it is my statement.

Signed Jesse Johnson Date: 5/9/YR-2

Jesse Johnson

Witness Joseph Lucey Date: 5/9/YR-2

Joseph Lucey

---

* This statement was given to Joseph Lucey, an adjuster for the defendant's insurance carrier, at the Johnsons' home on May 9, YR-2.

STATEMENT OF LEE MALLORY*

My name is Lee Mallory. I am 47 years old. I am married and have two children, both of whom are in high school. I work as a free-lance photographer and part-time as a school crossing guard at the corner of Mattis and Kirby. I have done that work for about two years. I work both in the morning and in the afternoon at that corner.

On the afternoon of May 8, YR-2, I was working on the southwest corner of the street. At about 3:25, I crossed over to the southeast corner of the street to reprimand a small boy who had not heeded my warning to stop. He had run out in front of some cars but wasn't hurt. As I knelt to talk to him, I saw over his head a man, who I later learned was Professor Fergus Williamson, cross the street from west to east in the crosswalk. When he reached the median, he suddenly turned south and began to walk south on the median strip. I then looked down to continue talking to the boy.

I then heard a thump and looked up instantly. I saw Professor Williamson being carried on the hood of a pickup truck about thirty feet south of the crosswalk. The truck stopped about twenty feet later. I ran over to see if I could help. When I got over to him he was lying on the ground unconscious. As I was running over, I had taken a small camera out of my pocket. I took a couple of quick pictures as I approached him. I really don't know why I shot the photos. I think it's just a photographer's instinct to photograph every unusual event. After I took the pictures, I went to him to try to help him, but other people arrived to help him and I realized I should return to looking after the children. I didn't want anyone else to get hit.

At the time I first saw Professor Williamson, I was also watching children on the other corner. However, I did see clearly all that I have said here. I did not come forward as a witness originally because I was upset and didn't want my story to hurt Professor Williamson or his family. I was finally contacted by the defendant's lawyer and told her what I saw.

I have read the above and it is my statement.

Signed ~~Lee Mallory~~ Lee Mallory Date: June 7, YR-1

Witness ~~Tracy Williams~~ Tracy Williams Date: June 7, YR-1

---

* This statement was given to Tracy Williams, an investigator for defense counsel, at Mallory's home on June 7, YR-1.

In an answer to an interrogatory propounded by the plaintiff, the defendant listed the name of Lee Mallory as a person who had knowledge of relevant facts. The plaintiff's attorney has discovered that Mallory was a school crossing guard on duty at the intersection of Kirby and Mattis on the afternoon of the accident. In a conversation with the plaintiff's attorney, Mallory said only that Fergus Williamson was out of the crosswalk at the time he was struck by Charles Shrackle's truck. Mallory refused to say anything more. The plaintiff's attorney received a copy of the above statement during discovery.

DARROW COUNTY, STATE OF NITA

Fergus D. Williamson, by and through his guardian ad litem, Wyeth Waring, Plaintiff,	)	
v.	)	Civil Action
Charles T. Shrackle and Shrackle Construction Company, Defendants.	)	

DEPOSITION OF ROBIN YOUNG

ROBIN YOUNG, called by the defendant to testify on deposition in the above captioned action and having been duly sworn, testified as follows:

Q: Would you state your name?

A: Robin Young.

Q: And your occupation?

A: Police officer for the Nita City Police Department.

Q: How long have you been employed as a police officer there?

A: About 4 years now.

Q: Did you know Professor Williamson or Charles Shrackle
before May 8, YR-2?

A: No, I did not.

Q: On May 8, YR-2, did you investigate an accident on
Mattis Avenue just south of Kirby?

A: Yes, sir, I did.

Q: What was the weather that day?

A: It was a clear, dry day.

Q: Describe the condition of the pavement, please.

A: The pavement was dry. The sun was shining. I didn't
notice anything unusual about the condition of the
pavement. There were no debris in the roadway.

Q: Describe the road where the accident occurred, please.
Was it a four-lane road where this happened?

A: Yes, sir, four-lane, two lanes each way. In other
words, two cars could be going south and two north at
that particular spot.

Q: With a median in between them?

A: Yes, a concrete median.

Q: Now, how wide is that median, do you have any idea?

A: I would estimate it to be about four to five feet.

Q: Could you determine from your investigation what direction was Professor Williamson traveling, from east to west or west to east?

A: I have conflicting reports on that. I have two people who state that he was eastbound and one who says he was westbound.

Q: Let's come back to those reports in a moment. Now, this pickup truck that was involved in this, did you ascertain who was driving?

A: Charles T. Shrackle was driving, and the truck was owned by the Shrackle Construction Co. I spoke to Charles Shrackle at the scene. He identified himself and his company.

Q: And from your discussion with him and your own investigation could you determine whether he going straight ahead or had just made a turn off of Kirby?

A: He was making a left turn from Kirby onto Mattis, South Mattis.

Q: And could he have been traveling at any excessive rate of speed?

A: I don't believe so.

Q: Was it your judgment that in the distance he traveled after turning the corner that it would be pretty hard to accelerate to an excessive rate of speed?

A: Well, yes, I guess so.

Q: Now, did he say whether he saw this gentleman or not?

A: No sir, he told me he did not see the man prior to impact at all.

Q: Are stop lights at that particular intersection?

A: Yes, sir.

Q: Did Shrackle have the green light or did he stop on the--did he have the stop light and then start from a stop?

A: He had the green light, but he had to wait for one car to pass before he made his turn.

Q: Do you know what color clothing Professor Williamson was wearing?

A: I believe he had on a running suit or sweats, a yellow T-shirt and white running shoes.

Q: Was he still at the scene when you arrived?

A: Yes, sir.

Q: And how far away were you when you received your call to go to the scene?

A: I was in the 900 block of West Springfield Street when they directed me to the accident scene.

Q: You were not too far away, then?

A: No, sir.

A: Was he conscious when you arrived?

A: No, sir, but he did gain consciousness just before the ambulance arrived.

Q: Did he say anything then?

A: Yes, he did. He seemed very disoriented. He was on the ground with several people gathered around trying to help him. He opened his eyes and said, "I just know we can work out a structured settlement."

Q: Did he say anything else?

A: No, at that point his eyes kind of rolled up in his head and he passed out again.

Q: And he was taken by ambulance to City Hospital at that time?

A: Yes, sir.

Q: Did you check the drivers license of the driver of the pickup truck?

A: Yes, sir. I ran a check on his drivers license and found no violations or outstanding warrants.

Q: Were there any restrictions on the license?

A: No, sir.

Q: And was there anyone else hurt in this accident?

A: No, sir.

Q: And was there any evidence of any alcoholic beverages being consumed by either party?

A: No, sir.

Q: Were there any passengers in the truck?

A: No, sir. Only the driver was in the truck.

Q: And what is his occupation? Did you find out that information?

A: I believe he's a contractor.

Q: Did he have work, south of where this happened, going on at the time—or do you know that?

A: I don't know where he was headed for, sir. I don't believe I asked him about that.

Q: Did your investigation reveal whether the pedestrian crossed at the pedestrian crosswalk?

A: I have one witness who says that he didn't, and I have two other witnesses who say that he did.

Q: Were these the only witnesses to the accident you identified?

A: Yes, sir.

Q: Do you have written reports of each of these witness statements?

A: I have given you a copy of the witness statements for every witness I interviewed.

Q: Is there any evidence—was there any evidence as to where he was—the point of impact, did you ever find out approximately where in the street that was?

A: I was unable to determine that. I looked for broken glass and other items, but there was none.

Q: Would he have had any occasion to have been south of that intersection? Do you know where he had been or where he was going?

A: I don't know, no. His office was west of that intersection, but I have no idea what his travels were.

Q: Did he have any children or grandchildren in school?

A: I don't believe he had any children or grandchildren in the school.

Q: There is a school on up there as I understand.

A: Yes, sir.

Q: Elementary school. Now, let's go back to the witness statements you took.

A: To clear up the witnesses on the accident. At the time I made out the report that you are reading from right there, I only had two, and one of them placed Professor Williamson out of the crosswalk and south of the intersection. However, the next day, when the newspaper account came out about the accident, I had another witness call in and state that the report was wrong. And I've taken statements from that witness and the other witnesses there, plus the fact that a gas station attendant saw him shortly before the accident. We took a statement from the gas station attendant also.

Q: And what did he say about Professor Williamson's position?

A: He said that Professor Williamson was in the crosswalk.

Q: And what is the name of the gas station attendant and his address, do you have that?

A: That's Pat Marshall's Texaco Station, at 1601 South Mattis.

Q: And this was Pat Marshall who gave you this statement?

A: Yes, sir.

Q: And the other statement was given by whom?

A: A Taylor Kelly, who lives at 1910 Elder Lane, that's E-l-d-e-r, in Nita City.

Q: Were either one of these people acquainted with Professor Williamson?

A: As far as I know, no, sir.

Q: Now, the person that gave you the statement that he was not in the crosswalk, what was--what was that name?

A: That was Taylor Kelly.

Q: And where does Taylor Kelly live and where was --

A: I beg your pardon, my mistake, I have to find my other statement. That was a Jesse Johnson.

Q: Where was Jesse Johnson when this accident happened, do you know that?

A: Jesse was in a car that was driven by her parent, Chris Johnson. The car was eastbound on Kirby at the time of the accident.

Q: And was the car west of the stop light or east of the stoplight?

A: At the time of the accident it would have to be east of the stop light, because it was--

Q: Jesse would have been looking back, then?

A: Yes, sir.

Q: Isn't that a little strange for a person to be looking back?

A: Well, that witness is only ten years old.

Q: Was there any other witness who put Professor Williamson outside the crosswalk at the time of the accident?

A: No, sir.

Q: The other two people are of age?

A: Yes, sir.

Q: And the person in Pat Marshall's gas station would be looking almost directly across the intersection--

A: That is correct.

Q: (Continuing)--from the gas station. Where was Pat in the gas station area, do you know?

A: Pat was at the western--or northwest bay area of the gas station at the time that Pat saw Professor Williamson.

Q: That would put Pat almost in a direct line with the crosswalk?

A: Approximately.

Q: (continuing)--more so than in the south bay, as I understand that gas station.

A: That's correct sir.

Q: Now, the other person, where was the other person?

A: At the stop light facing north on Mattis at Kirby waiting for the light to change, waiting to go on through the intersection.

Q: In other words, the other witness was south of Professor Williamson where he would go across the crosswalk, is that correct?

A: That is correct.

Q: In other words, this first report that was written could conceivably be wrong?

A: That's correct, sir.

Q: From your investigation, did you draw any conclusion as to whether he probably was in the crosswalk at the time of impact?

A: As I said, there were conflicting reports, but I believe he was in the crosswalk.

Q: Is that conclusion based on your conversations with the witnesses you have talked to since that time?

A: Yes, sir.

Q: Now, have you talked to any other witnesses that saw this?

A: No, sir, these are the only ones.

Q: Is there any obstruction in that particular intersection that could cause a driver not to see a person?

A: No, sir.

Q: What year pickup truck was this that struck Professor Williamson?

A: I believe it was a YR-9 Chevrolet Silverado - no, not Silverado - what do you call them?

Q: A Chevy, anyway.

A: Right.

Q: Would that have--did you observe whether the windshield was clean or dirty and is the visibility as good on a YR-9 as it would be on a later model, we'll say?

A: I believe the visibility is as good as on a later model and the windshield was pretty clean.

Q: Do you have anything further you would like to add?

A: No, sir.

Fergus Williamson v. Charles Shrackle, et al. conducted on January 9, YR-1, at the Darrow County Courthouse, Nita City, Nita.

Certified by:

Matilda Smith
Court Reporter

DEPOSITION OF CHARLES T. SHRACKLE

CHARLES T. SHRACKLE, the defendant, called to testify on deposition by the plaintiff and having been duly sworn, testified as follows:

EXAMINATION BY MR. JAMES (counsel for plaintiff):

Q: Would you please state your name, age, and address?

A: Charles T. Shrackle, 1701 West Johnston, Nita City, 32 years old.

Q: What is your business or occupation?

A: I'm a self-employed excavating contractor.

Q: And, is your contracting business limited solely to excavation?

A: Yes.

Q: All right. And, how long have you been so self-employed?

A: Since YR-4 . . . September of YR-4.

Q: All right. And, what is the name of your company?

A: Shrackle Construction Company.

Q: Is that a corporation?

A: Yes, it is.

Q: Who are the stockholders?

A: My wife and I. It's a small business corporation.

Q: What time did you arise on the morning of May 8, YR-2?

A: Six forty-five a.m.

Q: Is that your usual and customary time of arising?

A: Yes.

Q: Approximately how many hours of sleep had you had the night before?

A: Seven.

Q: Were you taking any medication or drugs at that time?

A: No.

Q: How was the state of your health on that date?

A: Fine.

Q: Would you briefly describe for us what you did that day prior to three o'clock p.m.?

A: I went to my office.

Q: Where is that located?

A: On Route 45 in Sommers Township, and started my crews working and then went to the corner of John and Holiday Park and worked on--at that--at that job for the remainder of the day.

Q: All right. And what was that job?

A: We were installing a sewer and putting the finishing touches on a sewer we had installed there.

Q: All right. And, how long did you stay at that job?

A: Until approximately 2:30 p.m.

Q: All right. Then, where did you go?

A: To Nita Builders Supply.

Q: Where is that located?

A: At 30 East John, Nita City.

Q: What, then, did you do?

A: Ordered some material, talked to the--some of the people in the office there and one of my men came in. I talked to him for a few minutes and then proceeded to Greenbriar Manor.

Q: All right. Now, you, at the time of this occurrence, you were going to Greenbriar Manor?

A: That's right.

Q: That is located on South Mattis Avenue?

A: That's right.

Q: How did you proceed from 30 East John Street to the intersection of Kirby and Mattis?

A: As I recall, I left Builders Supply and went to First Street and turned south to Kirby, and proceeded straight across Kirby.

Q: Okay. And approximately what time did you leave Builders Supply?

A: That would be difficult for me to say. I would say around three o'clock p.m. I don't--can't say.

Q: And, about what time did you arrive at the intersection of Mattis and Kirby?

A: That I do not know for sure.

Q: Did you go directly?

A: Yes.

Q: Did you have a job in progress at Greenbriar Manor?

A: Yes.

Q: What was the nature of that work?

A: We were doing some excavating work for sewer lines that were to be laid for an addition they're putting on.

Q: Was anyone with you at that time?

A: No.

Q: As you got to the intersection of Mattis and Kirby, do you recall whether the traffic light was red or green in your favor?

A: Green, in my favor.

Q: And, what were the traffic conditions at that time?

A: I would say moderate traffic. The intersection was busy.

Q: Did you come to a complete stop at any time after you entered the intersection itself?

A: No.

Q: Did you have to wait for any traffic to clear before you made your left turn?
A: I slowed for a vehicle that went by.

Q: Now, you were proceeding west on Kirby Avenue and were turning south onto Mattis?

A: Yes.

Q: And you would have been turning left?

A: Yes.

Q: From where did you start your left turn?

A: I'm sorry, I don't understand.

Q: Were you in the southernmost, westbound lane of Kirby at the time you started your turn?

A: Yes, I was, yes.

Q: And, did you make a gradual turn or sharp turn?

A: I made what I would consider a gradual turn to the east lane of Mattis--southbound on Mattis.

Q: And, did you have to wait for any vehicles to go through the intersection before you could complete your turn?

A: No.

Q: I believe you testified that you waited for one car to pass?

A: That--to complete my turn, you mean? I waited for one car to go through the intersection as I was approaching the intersection. That car passed through the intersection as I was approaching--I slowed down for it to pass through, I didn't have to come to a complete stop, just slowed down.

Q: All right. There was just the one car?

A: Yes.

Q: Okay. Did you observe any school children at or near the intersection?

A: Yes.

Q: And about how many children did you observe?

A: I believe three.

Q: All right. Where were they located?

A: They were on the corner of--it would have been the south--it would have been the southwest corner of the intersection--where the Texaco station is.

Q: All right. They would have been on the southwest corner, then, next to the Texaco station?

A: Yes.

Q: All right. And, were they standing or were they walking?

A: Standing.

Q: All right. Do you know what direction they were facing?

A: No.

Q: Did you observe a school crossing guard at that time?

A: Yes.

Q: Where was the crossing guard located?

A: The guard was standing on the other corner.

Q: On the southeast corner?

A: Yes.

Q: Did you see any other pedestrians at that time?

A: No sir.

Q: Do you know what color clothes the children had on?

A: No.

Q: Do you know the names of the children that you saw?

A: No.

Q: Mr. Shrackle, would you describe for us, please, what happened from the time you approached the intersection until the actual impact occurred?

A: Well, I approached the intersection and made the turn, and there was--there were cars coming from the west and I made the turn and there--and the impact and that was it.

Q: Do you know approximately where the impact--the first impact occurred?

MR. BARBER (counsel for defendants): With relation to what?

THE WITNESS: Yes.

MR. JAMES (counsel for plaintiff): With relation to the south curb line of Kirby Avenue.

A: I would say that--no, I don't know.

Q: Did you see Professor Williamson at any time prior to the impact?

A: No, sir.

Q: Did you apply your brakes at any time prior to the impact?

A: No, sir.

Q: What was the condition of your automobile at that time?

A: Fine.

Q: What type of a vehicle were you driving?

A: YR-9 Chevy S-10 pickup truck.

Q: And what type of license tags did you have on the truck?

A: Standard pickup truck type.

Q: And those are subject to inspection by the state of Nita?

A: Yes, they are.

Q: What is the date of the last inspection prior to May 8, YR-2?

A: I would have to check my records to find out.

Q: What was the condition of the tires on your vehicle at that time?

A: They were new--relatively new. They were purchased--I could check the date for you, but they were purchased not very long before. They had, I think, less than five thousand miles on them.

Q: And, had you had the brakes worked on at any time within the preceding six months?

A: Adjusted by myself, but that's all.

Q: And, would you characterize them as being in good working order?

A: Yes.

Q: What was the condition of the pavement?

A: Dry.

Q: And, the weather conditions?

A: Clear.

Q: Was the sun shining?

A: Yes.

Q: What did you do after--immediately after the impact, when you were first aware that your vehicle stopped something--struck something?

A: Stopped--applied the brakes.

Q: Were you able to observe anything at that time as to whether Professor Williamson went immediately under your truck or was thrown up in the air?

A: No, sir, I wasn't.

Q: Do you know approximately how far from the south curb line of Kirby that your vehicle came to a rest?

A: No, sir, but the officer has that measurement.

Q: Do you know your approximate speed as you were in the process of making your turn?

A: No, I don't. I would say around fifteen miles an hour.

Q: As you were making your turn, did you observe any automobiles stopped on Mattis waiting for the light to turn?

MR. BARBER (counsel for defendants): Where?

MR. JAMES(counsel for plaintiff): Either southbound or northbound.

THE WITNESS: Would you repeat that? I'm sorry.

MR. JAMES (counsel for plaintiff): As you were making your turn, did you observe any vehicles stopped on Mattis waiting for the light to turn in their favor?

A: Yes, I believe there were vehicles in the southbound lane of Mattis, waiting to turn, yes.

Q: All right. Did you observe any vehicles in the northbound lane of Mattis?

A: No, I did not.

Q: Had you consumed any alcoholic beverages on the date of May 8, YR-2?

A: No, sir.

Q: On that date were you covered by a liability insurance policy?

A: Yes.

Q: And what company was that with?

A: Boston Casualty.

Q: Do you know what the policy coverage was--the limits of insurance afforded by that policy?

A: I believe Mr. Barber would know that.

MR. BARBER (counsel for defendants): Go ahead. I'll find it for you.

Under policy FA 606560 and effective September 23, YR-2 to September 23, YR-1, automobile liability coverage of $200,000 per person, and $500,000 per accident. They have sent a letter to Mr. Shrackle advising him that the ad damnum is in excess of the policy limits.

MR. JAMES (counsel for plaintiff): As best you know, have you complied with all the conditions of the policy--

A: Yes.

Q: (Continuing)--required?

MR. BARBER (counsel for defendants): I have been advised of no policy defenses or-

MR. JAMES (counsel for plaintiff): The company has never indicated to you--

MR. BARBER (counsel for defendants): Boston has never indicated anything of that nature.

MR. JAMES (counsel for plaintiff): Did you have any other insurance, either a general contractor's liability policy or an umbrella type of coverage--

A: No, sir.

Q: (Continuing)--that would have--okay. Are you the named insured on that policy?

A: Yes, doing business--

Q: As Shrackle Construction Company?

A: Yes.

Q: Did you file personal income tax returns for the years YR-5 through YR-3?

A: Yes.

Q: And, did you file those either in Nita City at the proper time or in Memphis, Tennessee, at the proper time?

A: Yes.

Q: What was your approximate adjusted gross income?

MR. BARBER (counsel for defendants): You don't need to answer that. You can wrestle with me for that over at the courthouse.

MR. JAMES (counsel for plaintiff): I have no further questions.

EXAMINATION BY MR. BARBER (counsel for defendants):

Q: Mr. Shrackle, just to clarify some matters and pin it down here in the deposition, what was the first indication of the presence of Professor Williamson that you had?

A: The impact.

Q: Was it a noise?

A: Yes.

Q: Can you tell us or do you remember where the front of your vehicle was with relation to the sidewalk on the south side of Kirby when you heard that sound?

A: I was in the eastern lane southbound on Kirby, or on Mattis, rather.

Q: And can you tell us with relation to that sidewalk where the front of your vehicle was?

A: I was south of the sidewalk, I believe.

Q: And, when you say you were in the eastern lane, can you tell us, is there a median strip?

A: Yes.

Q: On Mattis?

A: Yes.

Q: When you were south of that intersection, where was your vehicle with relation to that median strip?

A: I would say about four feet over the median strip. Perhaps a little more.

Q: Four feet to the west of it?

A: Yes.

Q: Where did the sound of the impact come from with relation to the front part of your vehicle?

A: Left front.

Q: What did you do then?

A: Applied the brakes.

Q: When you say you applied the brakes, can--what did you do?

A: I put force on the brake pedal.

Q: What kind of force?

A: As much as I could.

Q: What did the vehicle do?

A: Stopped.

Q: What did you do?

A: Jumped out.

Q: What did you see?

A: Well, after--I moved around the vehicle and saw Professor Williamson lying under the--

Q: How was he lying under the truck?

A: Almost straight, with his head under the front bumper and his feet straight back.

Q: Was his head north or south?

A: South.

Q: His feet were north?

A: Yes.

Q: Was his body lying in a north/south alignment with his head south?

A: Yes.

Q: Was he conscious?

A: Not at first, but he did come to just before the ambulance came.

Q: Did you speak to him?

A: I spoke to him.

Q: What did you say?

A: I said, "Where did you come from?"

Q: Did he speak to you?

A: No. No. He was really out of it. I don't know whether he said anything to anybody else.

Q: What did you do then?

A: Well, the police arrived almost immediately. We got a first aid kit out of my truck and applied a compress to his forehead and then we waited for the ambulance to come.

Q: Did the truck leave skid marks?

A: Yes.

Q: Do you know how long they were or did someone else measure them?

A: The police measured them.

Q: Where was your truck precisely when it stopped with relation to that median strip, again? How far west of the median strip was it when it stopped?

A: I would--

Q: If you know.

A: I really don't know that.

Q: Only if you know. Did you examine your truck for marks?

A: Yes.

Q: What did you see?

A: There were some marks on the hood.

Q: Where were they precisely?

A: On the left-hand side of the hood near the division between the hood and the bumper--or, the hood and the fender.

MR. BARBER (counsel for defendants):I have no other questions.

EXAMINATION BY MR. JAMES (counsel for plaintiff):

Q: Mr. Shrackle, you mentioned a mark on the left front of the truck?

A: Yes.

Q: Would that be the driver's side or the passenger's side?

A: The driver's side.

Q: All right. Was your truck moved back shortly after the police or the ambulance arrived?

A: Yes.

Q: You mentioned that as soon as you heard the thud, you applied the brakes. Was your foot on the accelerator at the time you heard the impact?

A: I would--I could not say for sure.

Q: Was it on the brake at the time you heard the impact?

MR. BARBER (counsel for defendants): Tell him what your best recollection is.

A: My best recollection is it was on the brake.

Q: Do you recall why it would have been on the brake at the time you heard the impact?

A: Because I was going around the corner and I would have--my best recollection is it was on the brake simply as a precaution when you go around the corner.

Q: I believe you testified that the front of your vehicle was south of the sidewalk at the time you first heard the impact, is that correct?

A: To the best of my recollection.

MR. JAMES (counsel for plaintiff): I have no further questions.

MR. BARBER (counsel for defendants): Thank you, Mr. Shrackle.

This deposition was taken in the office of plaintiff's counsel on June 19, YR-1. After the deposition was transcribed, it was signed by the deponent, Charles T. Shrackle.

Certified by

Paula Brooks
Certified Shorthand Reporter
(CSR)

DEPOSITION OF WYETH WARING

My name is Wyeth Waring. I am a lawyer and a partner of the firm Williamson and Waring. I have been practicing law at that firm since my graduation from Nita University Law School in YR-10. I have lived in Nita City since YR-13. I am married and have one child, Charlie, who is one and a half. I was Fergus Williamson's law partner--and after his injury, I was appointed as his guardian ad litem. I have known him well both professionally and socially for the last twelve years. We are colleagues, but more than that we are close friends.

I met Professor Fergus Williamson on my first day of law school in YR-13. He was my Civil Procedure professor. Most of the students in my class were scared to death of him. He had an abrupt manner and a reputation as an exceptionally tough classroom teacher who would tolerate only excellent performance from his students. He was the kind of law teacher you would see in the movies. He had a gruff voice, an intimidating stare, and an incredulous style of questioning that would make students doubt their answers even when they knew they were right. He would also walk out of the classroom if students were unprepared. Still, everyone knew that underneath his crusty exterior, "The Ferg" had a heart of gold. "The Ferg" was really a law school legend.

He was born on April 1, YR-62. He attended Slippery Rock University, where he graduated with honors in YR-42. He then attended Columbia University Law School, receiving a J.D. degree in YR-39. He graduated number 3 in his class, editor of the Law Review and member of the Order of the Coif. Following graduation, he served as a law clerk at the United States Court of Appeals for the Second Circuit. He then worked in a private civil litigation practice until YR-35 when he joined the faculty of Nita University Law School. He was married and had three children, born in YR-32, 30 and 27. His wife died in YR-14.

In my second year of law school I began working for Professor Williamson as a research assistant. It was during that year, YR-12, that Professor Williamson began consulting on a part-time basis for a private law firm. Within a short time, it became clear that his particular skills and approach were in high demand. By my third year in law school, I was working for him almost twenty hours per week, and there was always more to do. In YR-10, the year I graduated, he decided to retire from teaching and devote full time to private practice in civil litigation. No one at the law school wanted to see him leave. He was one of the most beloved faculty--almost an institution. When he left, a group of his former students, including me, banded together to start a scholarship fund in his name.

He was absolutely sure he wanted to leave the faculty. By that time I was very comfortable working with him and he had confidence in my work. We decided to open the law firm Williamson and Waring. My role in the firm was to be the researcher and strategist. Williamson was the public persona of the law firm. I worked quietly behind the scenes.

The firm was an immediate success. Defending small businesses in civil actions became our specialty. The Ferg was formidable in settlement discussions. Something in his manner would cause opposing lawyers to confess the weakness of their client's position. We joked about his standard "no-money" settlement offer and how frequently it was accepted. It wasn't easy to ignore his low-ball offers because everyone knew The Ferg had no fear of the courtroom. He would take anything to trial--and very often win a case that everyone else thought was a dog.

From YR-10 to present the firm has been located in a downtown office building. We have a full-time secretary/receptionist, a full-time paralegal and a part-time bookkeeper. In YR-4, we hired a recent law school graduate, Courtney Majors, as an associate. Courtney Majors is an outspoken young attorney with a flamboyant courtroom style. Prior to the accident, I had talked to The Ferg about Majors. We both thought she would become a partner in the firm in the future. Williamson was planning to retire from practice at age 65. By that time, he thought that Majors would have established her reputation and would be ready to step into Williamson's shoes as the firm's public persona.

The Ferg had boundless energy. Every afternoon he took one of his legendary long walks. He would walk and jog for miles, sometimes working out case strategy ideas. I never knew where he went on those long journeys, but I know his workouts were very important to him. He was always coming up with new business ideas on those walks. One of his best walk-inspired ideas was ADR, Inc.

In January of YR-2, Williamson formed ADR, Inc. to provide Alternative Dispute Resolution services. ADR was something he had always been interested and involved in. He invited me to become a part of ADR, Inc., but I decided to let that be his baby. I was more than busy enough, especially with my baby, Charlie, on the way. The corporation was set up with Williamson as the sole shareholder. Williamson planned to continue to practice law at the firm and he hoped that his involvement with ADR, Inc. would only add prestige to the firm. He would continue as the law firm's "front man" who dealt with the clients and sold the work, but he would gradually hand off most of the day to day work to me and Majors. We planned to hire at least one more new associate soon.

In April of YR-2 ADR, Inc. was awarded a contract with Nita County to provide Alternative Dispute Resolution services for the judicial system. Although no one had ever contracted with the county, or any other municipality in the country, for these types of services, ADR, Inc. bid on and was awarded the contract on a fixed price basis.

The contract was a five year contract. It was to pay ADR, Inc. $3 million per year, contingent on ADR, Inc. being able to prove to the satisfaction of the County in a post award conference that ADR, Inc. had the facilities, personnel and financial capability to handle Nita County's Alternative Dispute Resolution needs. The post award conference was to take place in June.

When ADR, Inc. prepared its response to the county's Request For Proposal it did not create a formal business plan. But rather, Williamson estimated in his own mind based upon his years and years of wisdom what the costs would be and that at $3 million per year ADR, Inc. could make a "tidy profit."

When ADR, Inc. was awarded the contract, Williamson began recruiting and negotiating with former judges and associates to serve as mediators and arbitrators. One day after he had been making calls he commented to me that he was surprised at the rates and retainers these individuals were requiring to be paid before joining ADR, Inc. Even so, he was tremendously excited about the new venture. On the day of the accident, Williamson went to the 1st National Bank of Nita City in the morning. He obtained a commitment from the bank for a $1 million line of credit. Later that afternoon he was scheduled to go to sign a 5 year lease on the 52nd floor of the Cola Building, the most prestigious building in Nita City. Of course, he never made it there.

I was tremendously upset when I heard about the accident. His children really rallied around him and I hoped that he would recover and be able to return to his law practice. But, since the date of the accident, Professor Williamson has been unable to function as an attorney. His inability to process language has made it impossible for him to represent clients. Courtney Majors and I have continued to handle the cases that were already in active litigation at the time of the accident. Although we are both capable of handling the cases, I am most comfortable working in a "behind-the-scenes" role and Majors is still a relative newcomer to legal practice. Neither of us currently has Williamson's notoriety or his ability to attract substantial new business. His absence is a tremendous loss to the firm. It is a tremendous loss to me personally too.

This deposition was taken in the office of defendant's counsel on September 19, YR-1. After the deposition was transcribed, it was signed by the deponent.

Certified by

Anne Dolan

Anne Dolan
Certified Shorthand Reporter
(CSR)

---

* The transcript of Wyeth Waring's deposition was excerpted so that only the answers are reprinted here. Assume that this is a true and accurate rendering of those answers.

IN THE CIRCUIT COURT OF
DARROW COUNTY, NITA
CIVIL DIVISION

Fergus D. Williamson by and through his guardian ad litem, Wyeth Waring, Plaintiff, v. Charles T. Shrackle and The Shrackle Construction Company, Defendants.	)	AFFIDAVIT

AFFIDAVIT OF CAMERON SAWYER

I am Cameron Sawyer. I am retired now, but I used to work as a sportswriter for the Nita Journal. I have a degree in journalism from Duke University. I live next door to Professor Williamson and have known him since YR-15, when I moved into the neighborhood. Before his accident, Professor Williamson and I used to take walks together sometimes and we spent a lot of time talking in the backyard. We are both avid gardeners.

I was very worried when I first heard the news of Fergus's accident. I visited him in the hospital several times. I was glad that he had such excellent care at Nita City Hospital. After he was discharged from the hospital, he went to a rehabilitation therapy program. At the time, I was really skeptical about how much he would improve. I have been really impressed with how well he has done.

Since he has come home, I drop by Fergus's house almost every morning. At first, I began dropping by because I was worried about his being alone there. Now I drop by because I just enjoy it. Every day he gets up by himself, washes and dresses, and makes breakfast for the two of us. We eat eggs and grits and toast. Sometimes he even makes biscuits. I am still amazed that he seems to be able to do everything he needs to do for himself.

When I arrive, he always greets me with a smile and a "Happy sunshine morning!" He can't say very many words, but he is very upbeat. He seems to enjoy his life more than most people I know. As part of his physical therapy, he goes swimming three days a week. I often drive him to the pool, but he gets himself ready and is always the first one in the car. I think swimming is the part of his physical therapy that he enjoys most. He also continues to work on his speech therapy. I would not be surprised at all if he didn't recover most of his language in no time. He adds new words all the time.

His doctor has also encouraged him to do other physical tasks that he feels capable of. On nice days, he still works in his garden. His son and I sometimes help out with the digging and weeding, but he does most of the work himself. Last summer he had so many cucumbers and tomatoes that he took several baskets of them over to the law school to share with his former colleagues. I went with him once. Everyone was happy to see him. They hugged him and said how great he looked. the truth is, he really does look great. And he has a great deal of energy.

Fergus still likes to take long walks. Sometimes I go with him. Sometimes his son or one of his many friends will go. He children and grandchildren often come to visit. He likes to play board games with them and seems pleased to listen to the stories of their antics. He also likes watching "Law and Order" and "The Practice" on television. He probably would not like for me to say it, but he also watches reruns of "Seinfield." That show makes him laugh and laugh. He doesn't seem to have any pain or any anxiety. I do not believe that he missed his law practice much.

Cameron Sawyer
Cameron Sawyer

September 23, YR-1
Date

This deposition was taken in the office of plaintiff's counsel on September 23, YR-1. After the deposition was transcribed, it was signed by the deponent.

Certified by

Anne Dolan
Ann Dolan
Certified Shorthand Reporter (CSR)

September 23, YR-1
Date

McKellar Rogers, M.D.
544 Professional Building
Nita City, Nita 99995
(721) 556-0123

February 28, YR-0

Madden & James
Attorneys at Law
Suite 720 Nita Bank Building
Nita City, Nita 99994

RE: Fergus Williamson

Dear Mr. James:

You have requested a medical report covering my examination and treatment of Fergus Williamson. My initial examination occurred on May 8, YR-2. During his stay in the hospital, I saw this patient nearly every day. Since his discharge, I have seen him approximately twice a month. The following is a summary of my findings:

Past History:

The patient is 62 years of age and has been a law professor and practicing attorney since his graduation from law school more than thirty years ago. Before the injury of May 8, YR-2, his medical records indicate that he had been in good health. Medical history shows patient was treated for coronary arterial blockage with angioplasty in YR-6. Patient adopted low fat diet regimen and began program of exercise, walking and jogging. Cardiologist reported excellent results. Reports patient walking/jogging 20 miles per week continuing through YR-2. Non-smoker.

History of Injury and Symptoms:

Patient was hit by a pickup truck while crossing the street. Rendered unconscious at the scene. He was transported to the ER by ambulance.

At ER patient unconscious, not responding. Obvious swollen area at the occipital area. Started IV Normal Saline and sent Stat CBC, PT/INR, PTT, Glucose, General Screen and EKG. Suspected intracranial bleeding. CT scan ordered without contrast of head.

Rapid history revealed no history of stroke or prior intracranial hemorrhage, neoplasm, AVM or aneurysm. No acute myocardial infarction, diabetes or major surgical procedures within 14 days.

Rapid physical examination revealed abrasions and contusions to left side and back. Obvious contusion at left occipital area. Abdomen and extremities with no apparent injury. X-rays all negative for fractures or abnormalities.

Diagnosis and Initial Treatment

I diagnosed the patient as having an acute subdural hematoma, caused by bleeding between the dura and the brain. Following further examination and the results of the CT scan, I performed an emergency craniotomy, a surgical procedure during which the skull is opened to relieve causes of pressure inside the skull. Primary injury in the temporal area of the brain. This is the area of the brain which controls speech and memory function. Patient placed in surgical intensive care unit. Maintained with head elevated, fluid restrictions and continuous monitoring of vital functions. Various medications were administered to relieve intracranial pressure and prevent seizures.

Treatment and Progress:

Given the severity of the injury and the age of the patient, progress following surgery was remarkably good. Patient remained comatose for two days. On the third day, patient responded to his name, withdrew from painful stimulus, and tracked motion with his eyes. Fever onset at day three. Following an infectious disease consult, patient treated with antibiotic therapy. Neurological examination revealed mild right hemiparesis, continuing confusion, slowed response and loss of speech function.

After 6 days, the patient was afebrile and responsive; transferred from intensive care unit to the medical unit, where his medical management continued. Medical management involved a sensory stimulation program, physical therapy program, medication, nutrition, hygiene. Patient progress continued.

After four weeks in the medical unit at Nita City Hospital, this patient was released to a rehabilitation hospital for physical and speech therapy. Patient's mood was generally upbeat. Patient cooperative and worked hard toward recovery. Speech pathologist reports some progress in language processing, including understanding simple spoken language. Verbal responses limited to vocabulary of approximately 50 words.

On release of patient to home care, speech continues to be slurred and slow. Patient has great difficulty speaking and sometimes becomes agitated or confused in the effort. The voice sounds flat and hoarse. Patient experiences continued difficulty with swallowing foods. Following eight months of physical therapy the patient completes routine tasks without difficulty. He exhibits continuing mild loss of sensation and function in right extremities. Patient continues to need help with problem solving, making judgments and decisions. Ability to understand spoken language continues to improve.

Patient continues rehabilitative therapy and returns for periodic neurologic assessment. EEG conducted in Jan. YR-0 demonstrates continued focal slowing of electrical rhythms in the left temporal area.

Prognosis:
Predictions for recovery in traumatic brain injury cases are difficult. It is clear, however, that Mr. Williamson is unlikely to recover full function. The traumatic injury caused permanent damage to the area of the brain responsible for speech and memory. He will continue to suffer from difficulty with speech, reading and memory. He has also experienced some loss of sensation and control of his right extremities. I would not expect this patient to return to work of any kind.

Sincerely,

McKellar Rogers, M.D.

MR:kw

——————Electroencephalogram Laboratory——————

634 Medical & Dental Building ● Nita City, Nita 99995 ● (721) 556-2125

ELECTROENCEPHALOGRAM REPORT:

Name of Patient: Fergus Williamson

Examination Date: January 15, YR-0

Interpretation:

This is a standard 18-channel waking electroencephalogram. The background rhythms consist of 8-10 Hz medium voltage activity best developed over the posterior leads. This record is characterized by the appearance of arrhythmic 2-4 Hz activity over the left temporal regions with intermixed sharp waves. Occasional synchronous sharp wave bursts appear over both hemispheres and originate from the left temporal area.

Conclusion:

This is a moderately abnormal electroencephalogram indicative of a focal disturbance in the left temporal area. This finding is consistent with localized structural injury in the region of the left temporal cortex. The occasional sharp wave bursts raise the possibility of an epi-T form process. Clinical correlation is required.

WILLIAM J. MARTIN, M.D.

JBP Friedman, LLP

Accountants and Consultants
54 Madison Avenue, N.W.
Nita City, Nita 99903
Telephone: 776-923-4538

April 7, YR-0

Madden & James
Attorneys at Law
Suite 720 Nita Bank building
Nita City, Nita 99994

Re: Fergus Williamson

Dear Mr. Madden:

I am attaching schedules calculating damages in the Williamson matter. These represent my conclusions and the basis therefore. I would be happy to explain these matters further to you in person or over the phone. With any luck, however, this case will settle and we will not have to prepare for trial.

Wishing you all the best,

Paris Fisher

Paris Fisher

enclosures

Williamsom v. Shrackle

Assumptions used in calculation of damages relating to Williamson's income generated from Williamson & Waring:

1) Williamson would have retired at the age of YR+3.

2) Williamson & Waring would have been unaffected by Williamson's ADR, Inc. venture.

3) Waring and Majors have attempted to keep Williamson & Waring a viable law practice through YR-0.

4) Given Williamson's inability to practice law, Waring and Majors have decided not to continue with Williamson & Waring. Instead they have decided to join another law firm at the end of YR-0. As part of their agreement to join their new firm, Waring and Majors will be allowed to complete all existing files and keep the fees generated from those files. Waring and Majors have agreed to pay Williamson 65% of the fees generated from those files.

5) YR-2 revenue is considered to be unaffected by Williamson's accident. This is due to the long lead time associated with litigation. All of the files which were active at the time of the accident were handled by Waring and Majors. Given Williamson's inability to practice law after the accident, Waring decided to hire some per diem lawyers until Williamson was able to continue. These per diem lawyers charged Williamson & Waring \$50–\$100 per hour. These costs are reflected in outside services. The per diem lawyers charged between \$50 and \$100 per hour depending on their level of experience.

6) The Williamson & Waring lease will run through YR+3. Williamson & Waring will not be able to sublet the space and therefore it will be a continuing liability.

A

Williamson v. Shrackle
Summary of Losses

Item	Exhibit	Amount
YR-1 through YR-0	B	$385,437
YR+1 through YR+3	F	1,089,757
ADR, Inc	M	5,375,000
Total Losses		$6,850,194

B

Williamson v. Shrackle
Williamson & Waring
Calculation of Lost Earnings
YR-1 through YR-0

		YR-1		YR-0		
Projected revenue	C	$947,554	C	1,041,741		
Actual revenue	L	728,342	L	636,888		
Lost revenue		219,212		404,853		
Variable costs percentage	E	5.0%	E	5.0%		
Variable costs		10,919		20,166		
Lost profits		208,293		384,687		
Williamson's percentage		65%		65%		
Williamson's loss		$135,391		$250,047	$385,437	A

C

Williamson v. Shrackle
Williamson & Waring
Calculation of Projected Revenue

	Prior Yrs Revenue		Projected Growth Rate	Projected Revenue	
YR-1	$861,883	D	9.94%	$947,554	B
YR-0	947,554		9.94%	1,041,741	B
YR+1	1,041,741		9.94%	1,145,290	G
YR+2	1,145,290		9.94%	1,259,132	G
YR+3	1,259,132		9.94%	1,384,290	G

D

Williamson v. Shrackle
Williamson & Waring
Calculation of Historic Annualized Growth Rate

	Actual Revenue	Annualized Growth Rate		
YR-6	$590,016			$590,016
YR-5	693,408	9.94%	c	648,664
YR-4	631,605	9.94%		713,141
YR-3	813,271	9.94%		784,027
YR-2	861,883	9.94%		861,959

E

Williamson v. Shrackle
Williamson & Waring
Calculation of Historic Variable Costs

		YR-6	YR-5	YR-4	YR-3	YR-2		YR-2 (Adj)	5 Year Average
Professional Services		$557,588	$658,451	$598,756	$778,618	$825,663		$825,663	$683,815
Photocopy Charges		32,428	34,957	32,849	34,653	36,220		36,220	34,221
Total revenue		590,016	693,408	631,605	813,271	861,883		861,883	718,037
Outside Services	Variable	2,365	3,256	1,456	2,589	54,566	(1)	2,566	2,446
Telephone Expense	Variable	6,987	7,269	8,624	8,745	7,412		7,412	7,807
Postage	Variable	3,245	3,546	4,120	3,896	3,005		3,005	3,562
Courier Expense	Variable	7,963	7,412	7,832	8,654	7,452		7,452	7,863
Client Parking	Variable	7,863	7,265	6,854	7,569	6,542		6,542	7,219
Legal Research	Variable	6,354	6,542	7,235	7,588	6,622		6,622	6,868
Variable expenses		34,777	35,290	36,121	39,041	85,599		33,599	35,766
Percent of revenue		5.9%	5.1%	5.7%	4.8%	9.9%		3.9%	5.0%

B
G

NOTE: (1) Due to Williamson's inability to work as a lawyer, Williamson and Waring retained the services of other lawyers to fill this void. In YR-2 these fees totaled $52,000. Had Williamson not been injured, Williamson and Waring would not have retained these services.

F

Williamson v. Shrackle

Summary of Projected Future Losses

Projected income assuming no accident	G	$1,246,407	
Actual projected income	K	156,650	
Total future loss		$1,089,757	A

G

Williamson v. Shrackle
Williamson & Waring
Projected Future Profits
Assuming No Accident

		YR+1		YR+2		YR+3		
Projected revenue	C	$1,145,290	C	$1,259,132	C	$1,384,290		
Variable costs percentage	E	5.0%	E	5.0%	E	5.0%		
Variable costs		57,047		62,718		68,952		
Fixed costs	H	529,510		560,221	H	592,714		
Total costs		586,557		622,939		661,666		
Projected profits		558,733		636,193		722,624		
Williamson's percentage		65.0%		65.0%		65.0%		
Williamson's amount		$363,176		$413,525		$469,705	$1,246,407	F

H

Williamson v. Shrackle
Williamson & Waring
Projected Fixed Costs
Assuming No Accident

		Prior Yrs Fixed Costs		Projected Growth Rate	Projected Fixed Costs	
YR+1	J	500,482	J	5.80%	529,510	G
YR+2		529,510		5.80%	560,221	G
YR+3		560,221		5.80%	592,714	G

J

Williamson v. Shrackle
Williamson & Waring
Historic Fixed Costs

	YR-6	YR-5	YR-4	YR-3	YR-2	YR-1	YR-0
Salaries	$62,354	$68,742	$169,852	$182,475	$204,558	$228,223	$241,666
Bonuses paid	12,471	13,748	25,478	18,248	30,684	34,233	36,250
Health Insurance	6,987	7,562	11,265	13,698	15,004	18,236	21,456
Rent	78,000	78,000	78,000	78,000	78,000	78,000	78,000
Depreciation	9,875	10,258	14,698	14,698	13,224	12,546	12,546
Insurance (Equipment and contents)	4,698	4,888	5,623	5,896	6,258	6,644	7,123
Maintenance/Repairs	1,564	1,647	2,256	2,365	2,547	2,364	2,265
Malpractice Insurance	16,872	17,225	25,649	28,654	30,555	32,456	35,698
Brochures, Other printing	2,896	2,246	3,654	3,262	3,211	3,845	3,265
Directory Listings	2,888	3,214	3,241	3,696	4,122	4,368	4,568
Advertising	3,547	3,698	3,785	4,265	3,987	3,125	3,656
Charitable Contributions	2,000	3,000	2,000	1,500	500	500	1,000
Misc. Client Exp/Gifts	2,246	2,896	2,214	1,587	965	1,004	1,456
Entertainment	15,654	15,963	10,852	12,365	8,523	5,014	6,254
Seminar Expense	4,000	2,500	6,000	4,000	2,500	2,600	3,000
Bar Dues	3,500	3,600	5,000	5,500	6,000	6,250	6,500
Office Supplies	3,547	3,287	4,523	4,123	3,654	3,265	3,452
Miscellaneous Office Expense	1,245	2,369	2,589	2,211	2,589	3,896	3,265
Library Expense	11,689	12,785	13,564	14,006	14,789	15,698	16,325
401(K) Admin. Expense	3,500	3,750	4,000	4,500	5,000	5,500	5,750
Personal Property Tax	4,789	5,214	5,564	6,004	6,223	6,542	6,987
Fixed Costs	$254,322	$266,592	$399,807	$411,053	$442,893	$474,309	$500,482 H

In YR-4, Williamson and Waring hired a new full time associate. This new associate was the primary reason for the increase in fixed expenses. It is assumed that any future revenues generated by Waring and Williamson can be handled by the current staff. Therefore, the most representative years of Williamson and Waring's fixed costs are years YR-4 through YR-0. During that period, fixed costs increased at 5.8%. It is assumed that fixed costs will continue to increase at this rate for years YR+1 through YR+3. H

Williamson (65%) Waring (35%)

K

Williamson v. Shrackle
Fergus Williamson
Projected Actual Income

	YR+1	YR+2	YR+3	
Projected billings from existing Williamson & Waring files - based upon interview with Waring	$300,000	$150,000	$25,000	
Waring and Majors agreement that Williamson receive 65% of these fees	65%	65%	65%	
Projected Williamson income	195,000	97,500	16,250	
Lease obligation	78,000	78,000	78,000	
Williamson's percentage	65%	65%	65%	
Williamson's obligation	50,700	50,700	50,700	
Williamson's net income	$144,300	$46,800	-$34,450	$156,650 F

L

Williamson & Waring
Income Statement

	YR-10	YR-9	YR-8	YR-7	YR-6	YR-5	YR-4	YR-3	YR-2	YR-1	YR-0
Professional Services	$315,846	$337,008	$407,781	$447,743	$557,588	$658,451	$598,756	$778,618	$825,663	$698,231	$612,333
Photocopy Charges	21,375	22,346	26,479	26,054	32,428	34,957	32,849	34,653	36,220	30,111	24,555
Total revenue	337,221	359,354	434,260	473,797	590,016	693,408	631,605	813,271	861,883	728,342	636,888
Salaries	36,774	39,682	48,963	53,456	62,354	68,742	169,852	182,475	204,558	228,223	241,666
Bonuses paid	3,677	3,968	7,344	8,018	12,471	13,748	25,478	18,248	30,684	34,233	36,250
Health Insurance	4,563	4,965	5,560	6,254	6,987	7,562	11,265	13,698	15,004	18,236	21,456
Rent	42,000	42,000	42,000	42,000	78,000	78,000	78,000	78,000	78,000	78,000	78,000
Depreciation	6,783	6,783	7,596	7,596	9,875	10,258	14,698	14,698	13,224	12,546	12,546
Insurance (Equip and contents)	1,192	1,365	1,965	2,564	4,698	4,888	5,623	5,896	6,258	6,644	7,123
Maintenance/Repairs	1,145	1,653	508	1,456	1,564	1,647	2,256	2,365	2,547	2,364	2,265
Outside Services	1,056	1,369	1,896	2,269	2,365	3,256	1,456	2,589	54,566	74,125	78,556
Malpractice Insurance	11,807	12,635	13,054	14,876	16,872	17,225	25,649	28,654	30,555	32,456	35,698
Brochures, Other Printing	6,900	1,365	2,139	1,986	2,896	2,246	3,654	3,262	3,211	3,845	3,265
Directory Listings	2,069	2,206	2,534	2,789	2,888	3,214	3,241	3,696	4,122	4,368	4,568
Advertising	2,496	2,689	3,698	3,265	3,547	3,698	3,785	4,265	3,987	3,125	3,656
Charitable Contributions	1,000	1,500	1,000	1,250	2,000	3,000	2,000	1,500	500	500	1,000
Misc. Client Exp/Gifts	968	1,369	1,687	1,663	2,246	2,896	2,214	1,587	965	1,004	1,456
Entertainment	10,875	7,896	12,658	11,265	15,654	15,963	10,852	12,365	8,523	5,014	6,254
Seminar Expense	1,750	2,500	1,500	3,500	4,000	2,500	6,000	4,000	2,500	2,600	3,000
Bar Dues	2,240	2,500	2,750	3,000	3,500	3,600	5,000	5,500	6,000	6,250	6,500
Telephone Expense	5,717	5,986	6,352	6,588	6,987	7,269	8,624	8,745	7,412	6,453	6,005
Postage	2,982	2,156	2,541	2,785	3,245	3,546	4,120	3,896	3,005	2,475	2,245
Courier Expense	3,859	4,562	6,987	7,896	7,963	7,412	7,832	8,654	7,452	7,124	7,145
Office Supplies	5,698	2,635	3,456	3,654	3,547	3,287	4,523	4,123	3,654	3,265	3,452
Miscellaneous Office Expense	1,379	1,569	809	1,469	1,245	2,369	2,589	2,211	2,589	3,896	3,265
Client Parking	6,890	6,359	6,987	6,328	7,863	7,265	6,854	7,569	6,542	6,214	5,814
Library Expense	9,865	10,256	10,687	11,235	11,689	12,785	13,564	14,006	14,789	15,698	16,325
Legal Research	6,874	6,215	5,412	6,846	6,354	6,542	7,235	7,588	6,622	6,325	5,899
401(K) Admin. Expense	2,750	2,750	3,000	3,250	3,500	3,750	4,000	4,500	5,000	5,500	5,750
Personal Property Tax	2,760	2,965	3,125	3,698	4,789	5,214	5,564	6,004	6,223	6,542	6,987
	186,071	181,898	206,208	220,956	289,099	301,882	435,928	450,094	528,492	577,025	606,146
	$151,150	$177,456	$228,052	$252,841	$300,917	$391,526	$195,677	$363,178	$333,391	$151,317	$30,742
Williamson (65%)	$98,248	$115,346	$148,234	$164,346	$195,596	$254,492	$127,190	$236,065	$216,704	$98,356	$19,982
Waring (35%)	$52,903	$62,110	$79,818	$88,494	$105,321	$137,034	$68,487	$127,112	$116,687	$52,961	$10,760

M

Williamson v. Shrackle
ADR, Inc.
Projected Actual Income

Annual contractual revenue from NITA County	3,000,000
Projected costs	
Annual lease space 20,000 sq ft @ $25.00 per sq ft	500,000
Judges 8 judges billing 750 hours per year @ $200 per hour	1,200,000
Administrative staff 5 staff people @ average salary, including benefits of $25,000 per year	125,000
Furniture and fixtures Total estimate cost (approximately $250,000 amortized over the life of the contract - $50,000 per year)	50,000
Other miscellaneous costs (telephone, coffee, supplies)	50,000
Total costs	1,925,000
Projected profit	1,075,000
Number of years	5
Total projected profit	$5,375,000 A

Smith and Crabbe, LLP
Accountants and Consultants

666 Fifth Avenue
Nita City, Nita 99994
999.555.7777

April 15, YR-0

Price Pierce
Pierce, Johnson and Clark
Nita National Bank Plaza
Nita City, Nita 99994

RE: Williamson v. Shrackle

Dear Price:

I have reviewed the damage model prepared by Paris Fisher in the above referenced matter. In addition I have reviewed the depositions of Wyeth Waring, Courtney Majors, and David Penny – the 1st National Bank of Nita loan officer. Based upon my review of the previous mentioned information plus an independent review I performed related to small law firms and a review I performed relating to Alternative Dispute Resolution clinics throughout the country, I must take exception with many of the opinions expressed by Fisher.

Fisher in his/her assumptions states that Williamson & Waring will be unaffected by Williamson's ADR, Inc. This is not supported by the facts. Waring in his deposition states that prior to Williamson's accident, the firm was running at maximum capacity. Therefore, in order for Fisher to state that Williamson could devote a great deal of time to a new venture such as ADR, Inc. and continue to grow Williamson & Waring is simply unfounded.

If (and that's a big if), Williamson was able to obtain the Nita County contract for Alternative Dispute Resolution services, Williamson & Waring would have to hire 2–3 lawyers to replace Williamson and grow the practice as assumed by Fisher. Assuming Williamson & Waring hired one veteran attorney and one younger attorney in YR-1, the costs would be as follows.

The veteran attorney would require a salary of approximately $120,000 to $150,000 per year plus bonus and benefits. Williamson & Waring have historically paid a bonus of 10–20% of base salary to its employees. Assuming Williamson & Waring are able to locate a veteran attorney for $120,000 plus benefits of 20% of salary and the bonus is the minimum 10%, the total cost to Williamson and Waring in YR-1 is $120,000 plus $24,000 for benefits and $12,000 for bonus or $156,000. Given the current market for lawyers, it is assumed that these costs would increase at an annual rate of 10% per year.

The younger attorney would require a salary of approximately $70,000 to $90,000 per year plus bonus and benefits. Williamson & Waring have historically paid a bonus of 10–20% of base salary to its employees. Assuming Williamson & Waring are able to locate a younger attorney for $70,000 plus benefits of 20% of salary and the bonus is the minimum 10%, the total cost to Williamson and Waring in YR-1 is $70,000 plus $14,000 for benefits and $7,000 for bonus or $91,000. Given the current market for lawyers, it is assumed that these costs would increase at an annual rate of 10% per year.

The following chart shows the adjustments required to the Fisher analysis relating to Williamson & Waring.

	YR-1	YR-0	YR+1	YR+2	YR+3
Veteran Attorney	$156,000	171,600	188,760	207,636	228,400
Younger Attorney	$ 91,000	100,100	110,110	121,121	133,233
TOTAL	$247,000	271,100	298,870	328,757	361,633

Fisher assumes that Williamson & Waring will not be able to sublet its current space after YR-0. This simply ignores the current market conditions in Nita City. There is a shortage of space in Nita City. Not only could Williamson & Waring sublet its space immediately, it could do so at a rate more than its paying. Therefore, Williamson & Waring should show a profit. For purposes of this analysis, I have assumed that Williamson & Waring will sublet its space at its current rate.

Waring also testified that the new law firm he and Majors were joining would allow them to keep the fees generated from Williamson & Waring open files. Waring's deposition states that in YR+1 Williamson & Waring fees were expected to be $300,000 to $500,000, YR+2 were expected to be $150,000 to $350,000 and YR+3 were expected to be $25,000 to $100,000. Waring and Majors agreed to give Williamson 65% of these revenues.

Fisher's analysis assumes Waring and Majors would collect $300,000, $150,000 and $25,000. For purposes of my analysis I have assumed that Waring and Majors would collect $450,000 in YR+1, $300,000 in YR+2 and $75,000 in YR+3.

With regard to ADR, Inc., Fisher is way off base. First, it is unclear whether ADR, Inc. would have even qualified to receive the Nita County contract. The deposition of Penny states that although he gave ADR, Inc. a tentative verbal approval, it was contingent on Williamson providing personal financial statements and the approval of the loan committee. Due to Williamson's accident, these contingencies were never acted upon.

Even assuming that ADR, Inc. did receive the Nita County contract, Fisher is basing his opinion on Williamson's estimates of the costs. Williamson admits he never wrote a business plan but based his bid to the county on his knowledge and experience of the legal community. My research shows something much different with regard to the costs of such an operation as proposed by Williamson.

First, Williamson was planning on leasing space in the Cola Building, the most prestigious building in Nita City. And the most expensive. Fisher assumes ADR, Inc. will be leasing 20,000 sq. ft, but the floor plate of the Cola Building is 27,000 sq. ft. The average rent in the Cola Building is $32.00 per sq. ft. Therefore, the annual lease costs in the Cola Building are $864,000.

My research relating to Alternative Dispute Resolution services indicates that 10 judges will be needed for Nita County averaging 1,000 hours per judge at $225 per hour. This equates to $2,250,000 per year.

The costs relating to administrative staff, furniture and fixtures, and other miscellaneous costs all appear to be low. For purposes of this analysis, I will accept Fisher's values.

The following schedules show Fisher's analysis and my adjustments to his schedules. I conclude that Williamson's lost earnings are $0.

Sincerely,

Pat Daniels

Pat Daniels

Sched 1

Williamson v. Shrackle
Summary of Losses

	Per Daniels	
YR-1 through YR-0	**Sched 2**	$48,672
YR+1 through YR+3	**Sched 3**	$67,138
ADR, Inc	**Sched 6**	(1,695,000)
Total Losses		-$1,579,190

Sched 2

Williamson v. Shrackle
Williamson & Waring
Calculation of Lost Earnings
YR-2 through YR-0

	YR-1	YR-0		
Projected revenue	$947,554	$1,041,741		
Actual revenue	$728,342	$636,888		
Lost revenue	219,212	404,853		
Variable costs percentage	5.0%	5.0%		
Variable costs	10,919	20,166		
Costs to hire new attorneys	247,000	271,000		
Lost profits	(38,707)	113,587		
Williamson's percentage	65%	65%		
Williamson's loss	-$25,159	$73,832	$48,672	**Sched 1**
	========	=======	======	

Sched 3

Williamson v. Shrackle

Summary of Projected Future Losses

Projected income assuming no accident	Sched 4	$603,388	
Actual projected income	Sched 5	536,250	
Total future loss		$67,138	Sched 1

Sched 4

Williamson v. Shrackle
Williamson & Waring
Projected Future Profits
Assuming No Accident

	YR+1	YR+2	YR+3		
Projected revenue	$1,145,290	$1,259,132	$1,384,290		
Variable costs percentage	5.0%	5.0%	5.0%		
Variable costs	57,047	62,718	68,952		
Fixed costs	529,510	560,221	592,714		
Costs to hire new attorneys	298,870	328,757	361,633		
Total costs	885,427	951,696	1,023,299		
Projected profits	259,863	307,436	360,991		
Williamson's percentage	65.0%	65.0%	65.0%		
Williamson's amount	$168,911	$199,833	$234,644	$603,388	Sched 3

Sched 5

Williamson v. Shrackle
Fergus Williamson
Projected Actual Income

	YR+1	YR+2	YR+3		
Projected billings from existing Williamson & Waring files	$450,000	$300,000	$75,000		
Waring and Majors agreement that Williamson receive 65% of these fees	65%	65%	65%		
Projected Williamson income	292,500	195,000	48,750		
Lease obligation	-	-	-		
Williamson's percentage	65%	65%	65%		
Williamson's obligation	-	-	-		
Williamson's net income	$292,500	$195,000	$48,750	$536,250	Sched 3

Sched 6

Williamson v. Shrackle
ADR, Inc.
Projected Income/(Loss)

Annual contractual revenue from NITA County	$3,000,000	
Projected costs		
Annual lease space 27,000 sq ft @ $32.00 per sq ft	864,000	
Judges 10 judges billing 1,000 hours per year @ $225 per hour	2,250,000	
Administrative staff 5 staff people @ average salary, including benefits of $25,000 per year	125,000	
Furniture and fixtures Total estimate cost (approximately $250,000 amortized over the life of the contract - $50,000 per year)	50,000	
Other miscellaneous costs (telephone, coffee, supplies)	50,000	
Total costs	3,339,000	
Projected profit	(339,000)	
Number of years	5	
Total projected profit	-$1,695,000	Sched 1

IN THE CIRCUIT COURT OF
DARROW COUNTY, NITA
CIVIL DIVISION

Fergus D. Williamson by and through his guardian ad litem, Wyeth Waring, Plaintiff, v. Charles T. Shrackle and The Shrackle Construction Company, Defendants.	)	STIPULATION

STIPULATION OF THE PARTIES

By agreement of the parties, the expenses for care, treatment, and hospitalization incident to the injury to Fergus Williamson are stipulated to be $250,000. The amount stipulated includes actual past costs and the present value of continuing and future care.

APPLICABLE NITA STATUTES

Motor Vehicles — Chapter 89

Section 12(4). Right of Way. Public Roadways. Negligence

A. *Motor Vehicles.* The driver of a motor vehicle shall yield the right of way, by slowing down or stopping if necessary, to a pedestrian crossing the roadway within a crosswalk when the pedestrian is upon that half of the roadway in which the vehicle is traveling, or when either the vehicle or the pedestrian is approaching that half of the roadway so closely that the pedestrian is in danger.

B. *Pedestrian.* A pedestrian crossing a roadway at any point other than within a marked crosswalk shall yield the right of way to all vehicles upon the roadway.

C. *Negligence.* This right of way, however, is not absolute, but rather creates a duty upon the party having the right of way to exercise ordinary care to avoid collisions.

Comparative Negligence — Chapter 140

Section 3. Contributory Negligence No Bar to Recovery of Damages

In all action hereafter brought for personal injuries, or where such injuries have resulted in death, or for injury to property, the fact that the person injured, or the owner of the property, or the person having control over the property may have been guilty of contributory negligence shall not bar a recovery, but damages shall be diminished by the jury in proportion to the amount of negligence attributable to the person injured, or the owner of the property, or the person having control over the property.

PROPOSED JURY INSTRUCTIONS*

1. The Court will now instruct you on the claims and defenses of each party and the law governing the case. You must arrive at your verdict by unanimous vote, applying the law, as you are now instructed, to the facts as you find them to be.

2. The parties to this case are Fergus Williamson, who has brought this action through his guardian, Wyeth Waring. The defendants are Charles T. Shrackle and the Shrackle Construction Company.

3. Defendants have admitted in the pleadings, and you must regard as conclusively proven the following:

   - On May 8, YR-2, at around 3:30 P.M., Fergus Williamson was crossing Mattis Street when he was struck by a pickup truck driven by Charles T. Shrackle and owned by the Shrackle Construction Company.

4. Plaintiff claims that Charles Shrackle was negligent in his operation and control of the pickup truck and that his negligence caused Fergus Williamson serious injury. Plaintiff seeks damages for defendants' negligence.

   Defendants deny that Charles Shrackle was negligent or that his negligence caused Fergus Williamson's injuries. Defendants claim that Fergus Williamson was negligent, and that it was his own negligence that caused his injuries.

5. In this case, the plaintiff, Fergus Williamson, has the burden of proving by a preponderance of the evidence:

   (1) That Charles Shrackle was negligent, and

   (2) That the negligence of Charles Shrackle proximately caused the injury to Fergus Williamson, and

   (3) That the plaintiff suffered damage.

   The defendants have the burden of proving any affirmative defense by a preponderance of the evidence, including:

   (1) That the plaintiff, Fergus Williamson, was contributorily negligent, and

   (2) That the contributory negligence of Fergus Williamson proximately caused his injury.

---

* *These proposed instructions are applicable to this case only. They are borrowed or adapted from California, Missouri, and Washington pattern jury instructions. For general jury instructions, see those set forth after these instructions.*

Thus, each of the parties to this case has a burden of proof to maintain, and you are to determine whether they have met their burdens. Your task is to determine whether Charles Shrackle or Fergus Williamson or both, were negligent, and the extent to which their negligence caused Fergus Williamson's injuries.

6. *Negligence.* The terms "negligent" or "negligence" as used in these instructions mean the failure to use that degree of care that an ordinarily careful and prudent person would use under the same or similar circumstances.

7. *Contributory Negligence.* The terms "contributorily negligent" or "contributory negligence" mean negligence on the part of Fergus Williamson.

8. *Duty of Driver and Pedestrian.* It is the duty of every person using a public street or highway, whether a pedestrian or a driver of a vehicle, to exercise ordinary care to avoid placing himself or others in danger and to exercise ordinary care to avoid a collision.

9. *Violation of a Statute.* The violation of a statute, if you find any, is negligence as a matter of law. Such negligence has the same effect as any other act or acts of negligence.

   A statute in the state of Nita provides:

   (1) That the driver of a motor vehicle shall yield the right of way, by slowing down or stopping if necessary, to a pedestrian crossing the roadway within a crosswalk when the pedestrian is upon that half of the roadway in which the vehicle is traveling, or when either the vehicle or the pedestrian is approaching that half of the roadway so closely that the pedestrian is in danger.

   (2) That a pedestrian crossing a roadway at any point other than within a marked crosswalk shall yield the right of way to all vehicles upon the roadway.

   (3) This right of way, however, is not absolute but rather creates a duty to exercise ordinary care to avoid collisions upon the party having the right of way.

10. *Proximate Cause.* Proximate cause is that cause which is a substantial factor in producing the injury; it is a cause which, in a natural and continuous sequence, produces the injury, and without which the injury would not have occurred.

   To be a proximate cause of Fergus Williamson's injuries, negligent conduct by either Charles Shrackle or Fergus Williamson need not be the only cause, nor the last or nearest cause. It is sufficient if the negligent conduct acting concurrently with another cause was a substantial factor in producing the injury.

   Thus, there need not be only one proximate cause of Fergus Williamson's injuries, and you may find that the negligence of both Charles Shrackle and Fergus Williamson was the proximate cause of his injuries. On the other hand, you may find that the negligence of either of them was the sole proximate cause of his injuries.

11. *Comparative Negligence.* In the state of Nita, we have what is called a "pure comparative negligence" statute. The statute provides, as here pertinent:

> In all actions hereafter brought for personal injuries, or where such injuries have resulted in death, . . . the fact that the person injured . . . may have been guilty of contributory negligence shall not bar a recovery, but damages shall be diminished by the jury in proportion to the amount of negligence attributable to the person injured . . . .

What this means is that the contributory negligence of Fergus Williamson, if any, would not bar the plaintiff's recovery. The statute directs you to apportion the responsibility and, thus, the damages in accordance with the relative fault of the parties. Therefore, the damages allowed to be recovered by the plaintiff should be diminished in proportion to the amount of negligence which was a legal cause of the plaintiff's injury and which was attributed to the plaintiff, whether or not such negligence is greater than that of the defendant.

12. *Findings of Negligence — Percentage.* You are to determine the negligence, if any, of both Charles Shrackle and Fergus Williamson, and then to apportion the responsibility of each.

Please state your findings of negligence in the following form:

We find the conduct of the defendant, Charles Shrackle, was _____% negligent.

We find that the conduct of the plaintiff, Fergus Williamson was _____% negligent.

13. *Liability of the Shrackle Construction Company.* A company is responsible for the acts of persons acting on its behalf and for its benefit and purpose.

You are to determine in this case whether Charles Shrackle was performing duties for or acting on behalf of the construction company at the time Fergus Williamson was struck. If you find that Charles Shrackle was acting within the scope of the construction company's business at the time of the incident, then the company is liable for his acts; however, if you find that he was not acting within the scope of the construction company's business at the time, then the company has no liability in this case whatsoever.

14. *Damages.* In this case you must also decide the issue of damages. You must determine the amount which will reasonably and fairly compensate Fergus Williamson for the losses resulting from his injuries.

In determining the loss to the plaintiff, Fergus Williamson, you should consider the following factors:

(1) Expenses for care, treatment, and hospitalization incident to the injury to Fergus Williamson;

(2) Compensation for the pain and suffering;

(3) The present monetary value of the losses in past and future income due to injury and continuing disability.

15. *Life Expectancy.* In determining the amount of damages to the plaintiff, you may consider how long the plaintiff is likely to live, and that some persons work all their lives and others do not, that a person's earnings may remain the same or may increase or decrease in the future.

16. *Present Cash Value.* In calculating the amount of damages, you must not simply multiply the life expectancies by the annual damages. Instead, you must determine the present cash value for any award of damages. "Present cash value" means the sum of money needed now, which together with what that sum will earn in the future, will equal the amount of the benefits at the times in the future when they would have been received.

IN THE CIRCUIT COURT OF
DARROW COUNTY, NITA
CIVIL DIVISION

Fergus D. Williamson, by and through his guardian ad litem, Wyeth Waring, Plaintiff,	)	
v.	)	JURY VERDICT (Interrogatories)
Charles T. Shrackle and The Shrackle Construction Company,	)	
Defendants.	)	

The jury is to answer the following interrogatories. The foreperson is to answer the interrogatories for the jury and sign the verdict.

Interrogatory No. 1:

Was Charles Shrackle performing duties for or acting on behalf of the Shrackle Construction Company at the time Fergus Williamson was struck?

YES ____________ NO ____________

Interrogatory No. 2:

Please state your findings of negligence in the following form:

We find that the conduct of the defendant, Charles Shrackle, was ____________% negligent.

We find that the conduct of the plaintiff, Fergus Williamson, was ____________% negligent.

The percentage must total 100%.

Interrogatory No. 3:

Please determine the amount of damages to the plaintiff, Fergus Williamson.

Amount ______/______$

The percentage of negligence that you find to be apportioned to the defendant, Charles Shrackle (Interrogatory No.2) is multiplied by the amount of damages you determine (Interrogatory No. 3), and that amount will be the verdict for the plaintiff, Fergus Williamson.

The members of the jury have unanimously answered the interrogatories in the manner that I have indicated.

____
Foreperson